SOME OF IT WAS FUN

Some Of It Was Fun

by

W.E. Girard,
Lieutenant (Ret.)

The Pentland Press Limited
Edinburgh · Cambridge · Durham · USA

© W.E. Girard 1999

First published in 1999 by
The Pentland Press Ltd.
1 Hutton Close
South Church
Bishop Auckland
Durham

British Library Cataloguing in Publication Data
A catalogue record for this book is available
from the British Library.

ISBN 1 85821 682 6

Typeset by George Wishart & Associates, Whitley Bay.
Printed and bound by Antony Rowe Ltd., Chippenham.

*I would like to dedicate this book
to all who served in the armed forces
and to the friends and families of
all those who did not return.*

CONTENTS

Chapter One

BEFORE WORLD WAR TWO

I joined the Lincoln and Welland Regiment (Militia) in September, 1933, in Fort Erie, Ontario. Our Detachment was 'C' Company and our Company Commander was Captain Charles Muir. The Second-in-Command was Lt. Chalmers and Dunc Irish was Company Sergeant-Major. Most of the recruits were teenagers, but there were a few World War One veterans. One of these old soldiers, Jock Travers, had a son, Johnny, who was later with me in the Royals. We were issued World War One-type khaki uniforms, which included putties, wide web belts and greatcoats. We had to supply our own boots. I liked the uniform, especially the greatcoat, which was also good for duck shooting on cold early mornings. I might point out that at this particular point in time, the Militia was not taken very seriously or shown much respect in Fort Erie (nor in the rest of the country either). After all, it had been sixty-seven years since the Fenian Raid.

Lt. Col. W.W. Johnson, D.S.O. was our Commanding Officer and the Lincoln and Welland Regiment's Headquarters was in St. Catharine's, Ontario. We sometimes went to the St. Catharine's Armoury for target practice on the indoor range. We also used the outdoor ranges at Niagara-on-the-Lake. We were equipped with Lee-Enfield rifles and Lewis light machine guns. I had lived in Bertie Township most of my life, and had either owned or borrowed rifles and shotguns since I was ten years old.

Before that a neighbour's son and I had played with an old Fenian musket. I soon learned to handle the Lee-Enfield rifle, the training for which included firing with the long bayonet attached. It took a bit longer to master the Lewis light machine gun, which we spent many hours dismantling and putting back together before we were allowed to test it on the range.

In the summer of 1934 'C' Company joined the rest of the Lincoln and Welland Regiment for two weeks' training at the camp at Niagara-on-the-Lake. We slept in tents and were issued with khaki shorts. Our instructors were Sergeant-Majors from the Royal Canadian Regiment (Permanent Force). The Royal Canadian Dragoons (Cavalry) were also in camp, but I can't remember seeing any horses. I do remember that after our first drill session, most of us were suffering from sunburn, especially to the back part of our knees. It wasn't severe enough to stop us from having a ball game in the afternoon. We did four hours' drill each morning (with the usual ten-minute break each hour). Very few of us smoked, but it gave us a chance to have a drink of water. On the last day of our training we had a parade and an inspection, and were told how much we had learned in two weeks. In all it had been an enjoyable experience. I can't remember any complaints about the food, so it must have been okay.

During the winter of 1934-35 I attended at least two funerals of World War One Veterans at Greenwood Cemetery in Fort Erie. A few of us from 'C' Company supplied a firing party for the final salute to these veterans.

I left the Lincoln and Welland Regiment in the spring of 1935. I went to Montreal to look for work. I was born in Gaspe and had cousins from there who came to Montreal to work each summer, so I was accepted as one of them. I never learned to speak French, but I did learn to speak English like my cousins in Gaspe.

Chapter Two

WORLD WAR TWO – THE EARLY PART

When Canada declared war on Germany on September 4th, 1939, I was working on a turkey ranch near Dutton, Ontario. The agreement I had with the owner was that I was to be paid $20.00 a month, payable when the turkeys were sold in October. I had accumulated about $40.00 in back pay by September, when the news came. However, I made a deal with the farmer. I would settle for $30.00 cash if he would let me go and join the army.

On September 5th I boarded a Greyhound bus for Niagara Falls, where I stopped to see my girlfriend, Marie. We agreed to get married if I joined the army.

On Monday morning, September 6th, I hitch-hiked to Toronto to continue my army career. I had been to Toronto once or twice before and knew that the R.C.R.'s and the R.C.D.'s were stationed at Stanley Barracks near the Exhibition Grounds. Other than this, and my knowledge of the Lincoln and Welland Regiment, my information concerning the Canadian Military Establishment was rather limited. I did know that Queen and Yonge streets (Eaton's and Simpson's) was the centre of the city.

I found a recruiting station on Yonge Street near Queen Street with a large sign that read <u>JOIN THE R.R.C.'S.</u> They took my name and telephone number and said they would phone me. I had met a barber in a doughnut shop on Queen Street who worked in the summers at Crystal Beach, where Marie and I had also worked. He directed me to a rooming house on King Street, where I got a room for $2.00 a week. This included the use of their telephone.

By September 7th my cash was getting low, so I walked north on Yonge Street looking at the 'Help Wanted' signs in the windows. On Bloor Street near Yonge I got a job in a small lunch room. I worked the rest of the day, mostly washing dishes, and was given a hamburger and coffee and told to report back at eight o'clock next morning. I never made it.

When I got back to my room, there was a message for me: 'Call Sgt. Tingey of the R.R.C.'. I phoned first thing next morning and was told to report to the Fort York Armory. I was signed up on September 8th, 1939 and given Number B66590. I guess, due to the fact that I had been in the Lincoln and Welland Militia, I was issued a uniform (World War One type, without putties but with a white leather belt. I was one of the few that were being issued uniforms, while most of the others were given fatigue trousers and cardigans. I was told to report back the next morning in uniform. When I returned to my room, my friend from Crystal Beach went with me to a second-hand clothing store where he knew the owner. I was given a few dollars for my civilian clothes – my Sunday best.

I reported back to Fort York Armory next morning with my uniform pressed, buttons polished and white belt cleaned. I was told that I was going on Recruiting Duty at the North Toronto Glen Echo streetcar loop with another recruit named Cooper. The officer in charge of the Recruiting Station was a 'gentleman of the Old School', maybe Upper Canada College. His name was Captain McWhinney and he treated us like trained soldiers (which I considered myself to be). Cooper told me he was a mechanic and only interested in Army trucks.

I think we managed to sign up a few bumpkins coming from the sticks into the Big City, which was known as the Township of North York. I remember that Captain McWhinney bought us our lunch – fish and chips – on Yonge Street.

The next Monday morning the Royals started going out on the parade ground. Up till that time we had mostly been having lectures and watching the Toronto Scottish march in and out of the Armory two or three times a day. They always put on a good show. Our first drill instructor was one of the R.C.R. Sergeant Majors whom I had known from Niagara camp. He was a tall, rather lanky soldier, and quite mild-mannered for a Sgt. Major. He rode a bicycle to work and I was told that he had a large family. Nevertheless, I felt quite sure now that I had joined the R.C.R.'s. Somewhere along the line I must have learned the difference. It really didn't matter; I had plenty of other things to worry about – such as obtaining a marriage license. I had to try to get off parade a bit early to reach City Hall by 4.00 p.m. After a few attempts, I finally managed this. We had set the wedding date as September 30th in Niagara Falls. We still had to get a wedding ring, an apartment and a few other minor necessities. We bought a ring from Walter's, the Jewellers on Yonge Street, for $1.00 down and a dollar a week, because I was now considered as having a steady job. We were also able to get a small apartment at 260 Dufferin Street for $2.50 a week. Our Army pay was $1.10 a day plus $1.00 a day 'living out' allowance. We were allowed a small advance on our pay if we needed it, which most of us did. Sometimes Lady Kemp or some other kind soul supplied us with meat pies for our lunch.

On September 29th our first Pay Parade was held. The officer in charge, Capt. Aussie Young, made a little speech at the beginning to the effect that there would be no weekend passes issued for the coming weekend. I jumped up, saluted smartly and said: 'Please Sir, I'm getting married tomorrow,' which was Saturday. He replied 'Oh alright then,' and added: 'Don't anyone else try to pull that one on me.' I received a big hand from the boys, picked up my pay and my pass, and headed for the bus terminal at Bay and Dundas Sts. I always felt somehow that Capt. Young was responsible for any success I had in later life. He went on to become C.O. of the Royals – or was it the R.C.R.?

Our wedding was at a small Anglican church that Marie had sometimes attended. Our honeymoon was a stroll to the 'Glen' along the Niagara River.

We returned to our apartment in Toronto by bus on Sunday. Some of my wife's relatives in Toronto had thoughtfully stocked our cupboard for us. We had received a few wedding presents, including a chest of Community Plate silverware, 'Coronation' pattern, which we are still using. Our landlady at 260 Dufferin Street, Mrs Cowley, together with her daughter Gwen, were both very kind to us. Gwen worked for the *Toronto Star* and could get us passes to many shows and concerts. We got to see *The Wizard of Oz*, which was a big hit at the Imperial Theatre on Yonge Street.

Our life went along with no financial worries that I can remember. The Royals had moved into the International Building in the C.N.E. grounds. Our mess hall was the Martinique restaurant, which was not too far away. I had lost my 'Living Out Allowance' but my wife was now receiving married allowance, which more than compensated for the loss.

Marie had made plans to go to her home in Niagara Falls for Christmas. She had two younger sisters, Mary and Joyce, who were expecting her. I traded duties with a Royal who had small children and had been assigned to mess hall duty for the holiday. On Christmas Eve the Sgt. Cook (Murphy, I think his name was) gave me and another K.P. five dollars and asked us to try to find a large Christmas tree. We went up to King Street and west along to Queen Street, checking out all the lots that were selling trees. We found a tree that was much too large for a house – just what we were looking for. The vendor must have been an old soldier. He sold us the tree for three dollars and carted it and us back to the mess hall. So we each had a dollar in our pocket and the Sergeant liked the tree. We helped to decorate the tree with strings of popcorn and cranberries and whatever else we could come up with. While we were doing this, there were a few N.C.O.'s in their mess in one corner of the building. They were having a few drinks and singing 'Noel, Noel' and 'South Of The

Border, Down Mexico Way'. One of them was Sgt. Major Colin Barron, V.C. His nephew Johnny was with me in 18 Platoon a few years later. At the risk of being thought a 'name dropper', I must say that I am surprised at how many names I can remember after all these years. After the

mess hall was all tidy, we went back to our barracks. There was a party going on in our Recreation Room. Someone was playing the piano – Ray Leonard no doubt. The beer was plentiful and Major Eric Jones, our Second-In-Command, was leading the boys in 'Roll Out The Barrel' and other songs. .

Christmas Dinner at the Mess Hall was rather quiet. Not too many of the boys had stayed in barracks for Christmas. Some of our officers served us our dinner, and there was plenty of turkey and plum pudding for everyone. There was also a Christmas present for each of us from The Red Cross or the Sally Ann. After a quick clean-up, the Sgt. Cook told his helpers to take the rest of the day off. He would look after anyone who came for supper himself. It had been the first of many happy Christmas Days for the Royals.

Chapter Three

THE WINTER OF 1939-40

Some time before Christmas we had given the Toronto
Scottish and the 48th Highlanders a big send-off when
they went 'overseas'. Now the Black Watch (Royal
Highland Regiment) moved in from Montreal. They were
a very well-disciplined regiment, though perhaps not quite
as colourful as the Toronto Scottish or the 48th
Highlanders. We welcomed them and their pipes and
drums to fill in the void on the Toronto military scene.

There were not too many things out of the ordinary that
happened that winter. In the International Building the
'Dress of The Day' was announced over the loudspeaker.
Of course it was repeated by everyone and would usually
be slightly changed by the time we went on parade.
Greatcoats, balaclavas and Small Packs would sometimes
turn up as Tea Cosies and Large Packs – nothing serious.
One morning I was on Guard Duty at the Princes' Gate
of the Exhibition Grounds. We were allowed to have a
small fire in one corner of the concrete room beside the
gate. It was a very cold morning, and near the end of my
shift I was sitting on a tin can trying to keep a few coals
glowing by blowing on them. Suddenly there was a bit of

an explosion. It was strong enough to knock me off my perch and to scatter the hot coals and ashes all over the floor. I dashed outside to get some snow to cool things down, and then tried to clean the floor and myself the best I could. The hot embers must have expanded the tar that was around the edge of the floor. The guard who came to relieve me wasn't too wide awake yet, so I didn't mention anything to him. I also made a note in my log book that my shift had been uneventful. It was daylight by now and the new guard would have to stay outside, so I don't think he ever noticed anything unusual in the room.

On another morning I was on Guard Duty at the front of the International Building when a large limo with a flag flying drove by. I didn't give it a second thought until the Guard Commander came out and said: 'If that car with the flag comes back this way, give it a salute – it happens to be the Inspector-General. It did come back and I gave it a smart 'Present Arms', which I hope saved the Regiment's reputation. Up to that time I had only been saluting the 'Sally Ann' Tea Wagon when it came around on cold nights.

Also that winter I attended German language classes at Parkdale Collegiate with Glen Lewis and a few other Royals. Our teacher was a sergeant from The Royal Hamilton Light Infantry. He went on to be the Intelligence Officer at Brigade H.Q. I must have learned half a dozen German words, but never got to use any of them. The words I used to describe the Germans when I was wounded in Normandy were mostly Italian, which I had learned one summer while working on the C.N. Extra Gang.

I was on the Guard of Honour for the opening of the Legislative Assembly at Queen's Park that winter, also for the opening of the baseball season in the spring.

In February, 1940, after six months service, I was given two weeks' leave. We didn't do anything special except to go downtown window-shopping or to some of the free shows and concerts. By now we could even afford to ride on the street-cars, so began to see a bit more of the city. We thought Toronto was such a nice city that we decided to stay – as it turned out for the next half-century.

Chapter Four

THE THREE AMIGOS

From day one there were three lads in particular in 'A' Company who were always seen together. They were Privates Timleck, Edwards and Goddard. They all lived in the east end of Toronto, and Art Timleck's mother had been one of the winners in the famous Stork Derby. Art's parents held 'open house' for the troops almost every weekend and the boys from 'A' Company were always welcome. I don't think the Company Sgt. Major liked the idea of 'cliques' in his Company – he never seemed to be friendly with the Three Amigos. When we were in Iceland, Goddard took a photo of the Sgt. Major sitting on a large rock having a snooze while we were repairing a road. Goddard never showed anyone the picture until after we were in England and the Sgt. Major had returned to Canada.

Art Timleck had some relatives in England and they continued to have parties for the boys, though maybe on a smaller scale. I had left 'A' Company after we were in England, and had transferred to the 'I' Section, where I thought all those German words I had learned might be of some use. After that I more or less lost track of the Three Amigos.

I met Goddard after we had got back to Canada. He was working in Sunnybrook Hospital, where I was a frequent guest. He told me that Art Timleck had died in England but never mentioned Edwards, who I think didn't make it back. Later I saw Art's brother Bill at the Fort York Armory, where he was in charge of the Composite Stores. He remembered the parties his parents used to have for the boys, but didn't remember 'The Three Amigos'.

Chapter Five

ICELAND – LAND OF THE MIDNIGHT SUN

We had moved from the Exhibition Grounds to Camp Borden around the middle of May, 1940. We were under canvas, and spent most of our time being issued with new equipment. Each time someone returned from helping unload a truck, and someone else was stupid enough to ask what had been in the boxes, the answer was always the same. The boxes had all been stamped 'PITH HELMETS'.

The arrangement was that half the Regiment would be allowed passes the first weekend and the other half the second. I was included in the second half, and by the time my turn came, we were on our way to Halifax by troop train. I can still remember the crowds that turned out to greet us at every station we stopped at in New Brunswick and Nova Scotia. We made a brief stop at Quebec City, but I can't remember any crowds of well-wishers there.

We arrived at Halifax after a few days and went aboard the *Empress of Australia*, a luxury liner with four smoke-stacks (or was it three funnels?). The ship had not been fully converted into a troop ship as yet. Three of us were

16

assigned cabin 'C' on the third deck. I still have a souvenir from that cabin. Our escort, the British cruiser *Emerald*, was nearby with its signal lamps blinking steadily. I think the message was 'Let's Go - Let's Go . . . Canada.'

We finally did set sail, as they say in the navy, and seemed to be heading south. After about a week the air started getting chilly and we passed a group of rocky islands. Someone guessed that they were the Faroes. We were beginning to wonder if we would really need all those pith helmets.

We landed in Reykjavik Harbour in bright sunshine and the sun continued to shine night and day, with maybe a brief dip below the horizon now and then.

We disembarked on 'lighters', which were small fishing schooners, and set up our tents near the Radio Station on the edge of town. Then we all set about unloading our supplies, everything we were going to need for the next few months. I was assigned to guard one of the civilian trucks carrying lumber. The driver could speak some English and told me that he had a brother in Winnipeg. I drew him a sketch to show him that Winnipeg was the first town (of any size) west of Toronto. I also got him to understand that in the Canadian Army you never drive past a tea or coffee shop. I don't remember what the financial arrangement was, but a 10-ore piece was a lot like our dime. Sometimes we even got a cookie with our coffee.

The weather was, as the farmers in Bertie Twp. would say, 'too good to last' and it didn't. An icy wind blew in from somewhere, the north pole no doubt, and continued unabated for the next few days. Our main problem was that our tents were on volcanic rock, so instead of using tent pegs we had to pile stones on the tent lines.

After a few weeks, 'A' Company was moved to Alafoss, about twenty miles out of town. It was a fishing village with a few smelly drying sheds and not much else. There was a nice swimming pool, where a hot stream and a cold stream joined. There were other pools of bubbling hot water. One lad tried putting his laundry in a bag and dropping it in one of these pools. When he checked it after about ten minutes, all that was left was the cord that had held the bag.

We patrolled the nearby beaches night and day, and took the odd shot at the rooks (oversized crows) that strutted along the beach saying 'awk, awk, awk'. We finally convinced them that there was plenty of room for all of us, and that they could have all the dead fish that washed up on the shore.

We were issued with long sheepskin coats for the beach patrol. I had my picture taken wearing one on a warm day, when I really didn't need it. Sometimes at night it did get quite cool even in July. There was a rumour around that someone had shot a ram, and that he had got off with only a fine. His defence was that the animal had charged at him and he had shot it in self-defence. While some of the sheep did have horns, none of the ones I saw looked that fierce.

There was a low mountain near our camp with a sort of concave swampy area on top, so I was told. We had a lookout post up there and sent a patrol up every day. I had never been picked for this patrol – my policy was never to complain about duties and never to volunteer. I had heard all about the stiff climb up the mountain many times. Some time in October my turn came. I wanted to be in good shape for the climb, and as I had a bit of a sore throat, I went on sick parade the day before. Right away

the Sergeant and all the rest said I was 'swinging the lead' to avoid the patrol. It just so happened that the medical orderly on duty was an old friend of mine and he didn't have many other customers. He decided to put me to bed in the medical tent for a day or two. That evening the sergeant dropped by to say he was sorry and that he hoped that I would survive. By the time my name came up again for the patrol, we were on our way to Scotland. I did have another similar experience, but that will be another story.

One of our other duties was to keep an eye open on a power station and dam about ten miles up a river from our camp. We were told it had been built by Sweden and it was quite modern. There were bus tours from Reykjavik stopping to see it – mostly sailors. From the dam you could see Mt. Hekla (non-active) with eagles circling around it.

We made a daily patrol to the power station by army truck, starting at a lake that had a small hotel nearby. On our way out on the patrol, we stopped at the hotel and ordered our lunch to be ready when we returned in about four hours. The Army wasn't paying for our lunch – not directly anyway. The patrol was uneventful and when we arrived back at the hotel, our lunch was ready, served in a large blue willow-pattern dish. It was wild duck or something, not fish or mutton, and it sure tasted good to us. The hotel's only claim to fame was that some Italians (Balbo, I think), who were crossing the Atlantic by seaplane, had stopped here. They had plenty of photos of this event on display at the hotel. This was the nicest area that we visited in Iceland. The worst – well, you could take your pick – maybe the top of that mountain.

There was a bus line between Alafos and Reykjavik and we were allowed a pass to town once a week. The Flags Hotel – so named by the Royals – was a good place to have a meal. There was usually stew on the menu, but not mutton stew. There were not many cows on the island, but plenty of ponies. All we ever stipulated was that we didn't want mutton. Near the end of our stay the road to town would be clogged with sheep that were streaming down from the hills for the winter. The ride would take much longer, but eventually we would get to town. There was one nice swimming pool in Reykjavik. A pipe-line was under construction leading from some hot springs to town. It had been started by some Germans and was possibly completed by Royal Engineers. We had a Royal named Smittagard, a Dane, who could converse with the locals. He could buy almost anything you wanted – for a price, including the local drink called 'Black Death'. I never tried it. Near the Flags Hotel was a statue of a Viking – Eric The Red, or Lief The Lucky, quite a fierce looking warrior-of-old. It made us look like Boy Scouts.

The Royal Marines had a camp-site near ours. They were installing coastal batteries. Our C.O. got friendly with theirs, and when we were in England, the Band of The Royal Marines came and played for us on our 'Mount Sorel Day' parade and picnic.

Near a swimming pool that we were allowed to use near Alafoss was some sort of woollen mill. It was staffed by orphans, who also attended educational classes. Their teacher was a pretty girl with red hair from Scotland. Pantaleo, a big lad from Forest Hill, was quite friendly with her. After the war I heard that Pantaleo had joined the Forest Hill Police, but I never heard any more about the teacher.

There was one airport on the island, and a few 'Soccer

fields' that could have been used as landing strips. Their goals were about a quarter of a mile apart. The only military aircraft we saw were one or two Fairy Battle light bombers. They must have been used for submarine detection patrols. Sometimes a 'Short Sunderland' flying boat would land in the harbour bringing mail from England. There was a bit more activity in the skies when we reached England in late 1940. We had to start taking Aircraft Identification courses.

We left Iceland in October, again on the *Empress of Australia*, which was now fully converted into a troopship. It was a much stormier trip but we landed in Gourock, Scotland, a few days later. We had a good view of the hundreds of ships in the Clyde Estuary, where some of the convoys used to be assembled.

Chapter Six

SPORTS IN THE ARMY

Golf was the only sport that I was really interested in. I liked swimming also and had joined a boxing club while in high school in Fort Erie. I tried boxing in the Army and went three rounds with Ken Howard, a middleweight who went on to be champion of the Second Division. He was at least twenty pounds heavier than I was, but I was taller and had a longer reach. I had been warned that he had a good left hook, as well as a rather mean disposition. I managed to last three rounds by keeping him off balance with left jabs and by setting the pace – my legs were in good shape. But I could see that boxing wasn't really my sport.

I got interested in cross-country running in England. On our weekly sports afternoon we would be taken by lorry ten miles or more out into the country. We would be pointed in the general direction of our camp and it would take two hours or more to get back at our own pace, across hill and dale. If there just happened to be a bus going our way – and it was a cold day – we might hop on for a mile or two. If it was a warm day, we might even stop at a pub for a quick pint. When we reached our camp, we would have a shower and could then have the rest of the day off.

Another chap, Grandpapa Gill (he was a year or two older than most of us), and I decided to go on to the Brigade and Divisional Sports Meets. It meant a bit of time off for training and a trip to some nearby park for the events. We never managed to win any prizes in the sports but I did manage to win a few quid in the crap games we had after the sports were finished. A crap game at the divisional level was quite an event for a country boy. At one crap game I wasn't having any luck and lost my bankroll (about ten shillings). A friend of mine, Cameron Lithcott, insisted on lending me ten bob, which I also lost. I don't remember ever paying him back, but maybe I'll meet him again some time. He was from one of the Caribbean Islands and would join in with the English lads playing cricket. I would sometimes join in with him – but only for the tea break. I went to White City Stadium to see the Canadian and American teams play football. Bill Lloyd from the Royals played in the first game and the Canadian team won. The second game was a different story. The Americans showed up with mostly 'pro' football players in their line-up and easily won the game by a wide margin.

Did I say I was interested in golf? On my first leave, November, 1940, I played a few rounds at the Braid Hills Golf Course near Edinburgh. It was quite a nice course, a bit rugged by Canadian standards. You could rent a set of clubs for a shilling. At that time the golf course was also being used as a site for Smudge Pots, which put up a smoke screen to protect the Firth of Forth Bridge. There were several air raid warnings while I was there, but the bridge was never damaged.

On another leave I went to St. Andrews and played the Old Course. I still have my score card. I didn't break any records, but it was good just to see such a famous golf course. The Scottish ale in the club house was also very good. I played another course at North Berwick but can't remember much about it.

Back in England, at Camberley, near Sandhurst, I decided to check out the golf situation. I found out that the Red Cross had made arrangements for Canadians to play at the Royal Sussex Golf Club nearby. Up to that time only the officers had been informed of this, but I found out that there were no restrictions as to rank. I knew another private who had been an assistant 'pro' at a course near Toronto and after a few practice rounds we entered a tournament being run by some of our officers. If you were going to be away from camp at lunch time, and you talked nicely to the Sgt. Cook, he would come up with a cheese sandwich or two. Back at the Golf Club we stopped for lunch and were able to buy a drink. I tried Bulmers' Champagne Cider. It was a warm day and the cider came in a rather small bottle. As the cheese sandwich was rather dry, I decided to try another bottle. When we resumed play after lunch, I could see three balls every shot I played. I tried hitting the one in the middle and after a few holes it was okay. I didn't win any prizes and didn't drink any more cider that day. There was a mini-golf (putting) course in a park in Camberley which I played a few times.

In the summer of 1942 we were on the Isle of Wight for Special Training. We were in a Butlins Holiday Camp at a place called Brambles Chine. Another private and I were in a cabin with an older soldier, Cpl. McDonald. We called him Bonnie Mac. The first part of our training was called Unarmed Combat. Corporal McDonald sprained a shoulder muscle on the first day. On the second he came on parade with one arm in a sling. We promptly changed the name of the training to 'One-Armed' Combat to suit

26

the occasion. After training we were allowed to go swimming in the surf. There was also a mini-golf course nearby. It was quite a nice course with natural grass greens. It was near Tennison's Cottage, which boasted a typical Olde English Garden. Quite a picturesque setting. Jim Vincent and I played this course almost every evening while we were on the Isle of Wight. After I had returned home, we lived near Sunnyside Park, which also had a mini-golf layout. The first time I played it, guess who I met? Jim Vincent of course. So we played a few rounds and talked over our summer on the Isle of Wight. We had walked over most of the Island, climbed hundreds of steps at Ventnor, practiced a few forced marches, and still had time for golf. It had been quite a pleasant summer.

Chapter Seven

WHAT EVER HAPPENED TO DONALD MINNIE? DON'T ASK ME!

I knew Donald Minnie from way back – maybe in old 'A' Company or even before the companies were formed. He was a little guy, quite mild mannered and soft spoken, with sallow complexion, pale gray eyes and sandy coloured hair. I'm sure I couldn't describe him if I hadn't seen him on a daily basis over a long period.

Donald disappeared from camp some time after we were in England. I asked several people I had joined up with or from 'A' Company if they had any idea what had happened to Donald. Nobody seemed to know just who the hell I was looking for. I checked and found that he was listed as Absent Without Leave in the official regimental records.

Donald came back to the Regiment one day between two big Military Police. He was wearing 'civvies' and carrying a ration card, not in his name – maybe he called himself Donald Duck. He could have strolled around our camp all day and I'm sure he would never have been noticed. Donald was issued a new uniform, including dog-tags, and received fourteen days 'Confined to Barracks' as punishment.

Donald disappeared again after serving his fourteen days. Once again there wasn't anybody I knew who could remember anything about him. After a few weeks he was brought back by two 'Limey' Military Police in their red hats. He was again in civvies and also wearing hand-cuffs. He must have been getting a reputation. Donald was awarded twenty-eight days in the Canadian Military Prison at Hedley Downs, but didn't arrive there for a while. He disappeared from our Guard House. The only thing that could be determined was that he must have slipped away at a time when the Sergeant was alone with him. At all other times there had been at least two guards watching him. Donald eventually reached Hedley Downs and the rest of us Royals made a dry, unopposed landing at Juno Beach in Normandy, about a month after 'D' Day.

We were busily engaged removing the water-proofing from our bren carriers when I happened to notice a little guy sitting on a pile of boxes nearby. He was wearing a wedge cap and had a rifle slung over one shoulder. He may have been smoking a cigarette. You've guessed it – it was none other but Donald Minnie. Hedley Downs had sent their entire compliment of guests to help unload the supply ships. Donald was guarding the supplies that had been landed – sort of minding the store while the rest of his crew had returned to the ship in a landing craft for more. This was rather like leaving the fox to guard the hen house.

After a brief chat about old times at the Exhibition Grounds, I said, 'See you in Paris' and returned to my task in hand. I wondered if Donald would still be there when his crew returned.

I never did get to Paris, but if I had, I would have kept an eye out for Donald – dressed in civvies and wearing a blue beret, and more than likely 'parlee-vooing'.

I could never find Donald's name in any casualty lists, so I hope he survived. He was the kind of person that if you and he were the last two persons on a subway train late at night, when you reached the last stop, you would be alone. Furthermore, you would not be able to remember if there really had been someone else with you or what he looked like.

I suppose Donald, or his spirit, are somewhere minding their own business so I guess I should do the same – at last. So I'll just say 'Goodbye Donald' for now, but I wouldn't bet on my not meeting him again some time.

Chapter Eight

HOW TO HUSTLE A FEW BOB IN THE ARMY

Eisenhower Jackets & Other 'Flogables'

One day an American Military Police sergeant on a large Harley-Davidson bike rode into our camp. He asked the first Royal he saw: 'Do you all have any Eisenhower Jackets you would like to sell?' That is what the Yanks called the top part of our battle dress. He would pay $5.00 U.S. for any jacket in reasonable shape. I was a bit surprised at just how many spare jackets there seemed to be around camp. I still had the first one with which I had been issued. I kept it for wearing when I went on leave and didn't want to sell it. There were plenty of others who did sell their old jackets.

The Americans were also always looking for dress shirts and neckties. I sold one or two extra ones that I had. One of our lads had a nice new dress shirt and tie which he kept to wear on leave. He came back wearing a beat-up old A.T.S. shirt and tie. His friend had left while he was still asleep. We told him he should have sold his shirt to the Yanks.

We could also sometimes make trades with the Americans. We liked their fatigue uniform tops. They were green denim with short sleeves – quite sporty. Some of the boys would wear them around camp when not on duty – anything to be different. If an officer asked why you were wearing it, you would just say: 'New Issue, sir'. That would keep him quiet at least until he could check it out. Most of our officers had more important things to think about at that time.

Blankets were always saleable, to be made into blanket coats. There were never too many spare blankets around, and it was the light coloured ones especially that were in demand. The trick was to find an old discarded blanket and try to get it replaced with a new one.

The Air Raid Wardens and other civilians who had to spend a lot of time standing around in the cold were always looking for Red Cross pyjamas and socks. We would never charge them more than a few bob – which, after all, was all profit.

If you really wanted to earn a little extra cash you could always work on the local farms. On one occasion another chap and I worked for a week for a farmer near Winchelsea, cutting small trees. He arranged for us to stay with one of his tenants. The man was a shepherd and his wife had lived in Canada's West for a few years. They tried to make us feel at home. We would take a sandwich with us and go to the wood lot where we worked each morning. We used what we call broad axes, and were only expected to cut down the smaller trees. We would start a small fire to burn the branches. It must have been in September because there were plenty of apples around, which we would roast in our fire to have with our sandwich. We would also make tea in a tin can. The farmer was pleased with our work, and at the end of the week paid us each five quid. That was enough to go on a holiday for the next week. Some of our boys worked almost every time they went on leave. The large breweries in Manchester seemed to be the most popular place to work – cash plus a few beers each day. I never got around to trying it.

One chap I knew spent his weekends pressing uniforms and shirts for a shilling or two. He had one of the few irons in camp and would never let anyone borrow it. It could never be said that the Canadians flashed their money as the Yanks did. This made it bad for the other servicemen, like paying half a crown for a shoeshine instead of sixpence. After having gone through 'The Depression' in Canada, most of us were quite close with a buck or a quid.

Chapter Nine

GHOSTS ON PARADE

When we were stationed at Denne Park near Horsham, there was a pub across the road called The Fox and Hounds – the actual name. Most of the pubs had been re-named by the Canadians. For instance 'Bunch of Grapes' in the Strand was now 'The Grapes of Wrath'. Or another pub called the 'Three Rooks' was now the 'Four Crows'. There was one pub near Bognor Regis that defied our attempts to re-name it. It was called 'The Shoulder of Lamb and Cucumbers' – we just couldn't top that one.

To get back to our ghost story, some of the boys would duck over to the Fox and Hounds at lunch time and rush back just before 'Fall In' sounded. In the Carrier Platoon we wore black coveralls most of the time. There was some sort of mill across from the pub with a fence on either side. Most of the time there would be a wagon in the passageway either loading or unloading – or maybe off-loading. There was a pit under the wagon for the sweepings – flour or whatever was spilled. There was still plenty of room on either side of the wagon to get to our parade ground if you were careful. On this particular day we were two men short on 'Fall In' and there wasn't any wagon at the mill. Suddenly, as we were answering the roll call, these two ghosts came dashing across the parade ground and fell in at the end of the line. They had lingered somewhat too long over their beers and in their mad dash to get back had smothered themselves in flour. There was

a bit of laughter in the ranks but all the Sergeant said was: 'Looks like we have a couple of ghosts on parade today.' As it so happened, they were both named Young and their names were near the end of the roster and hadn't been called yet. That expression 'Ghosts on Parade' was also used if someone tried using a bit of talc instead of shaving.

We also had a Sgt. Lyall Young in the Carrier Platoon and I think he received a medal for some brave deed in Normandy or Holland.

Chapter Ten

THE PADRE'S TOUR

Every now and then our padre, Captain Appleyard, would announce that he would be conducting a tour of a famous church or cathedral on a certain weekend. If you were interested in going, you just put your name on a list in his office and he would let you know the exact date. Usually there would be ten or twelve of us who wanted to go. This would be enough for one truck to accommodate.

I chose to go on the tour of Exeter Cathedral in Devon. At this time we were stationed on the south coast, possibly at Littlehampton. It wasn't too far for us to drive to Exeter.

We arrived at the city of Exeter around noon on a Saturday, to be greeted by the Mayor, who was decked out in his official chain of office for the occasion. He took us for lunch and then on a personally conducted tour of the city. On Saturday evening we were guests at a party held in a school gymnasium. They even managed to find some hot dogs for refreshments. The Mayor must have made friends with some Americans.

On Sunday morning we attended the service at the Cathedral and were then taken on a tour of the building by the Dean of Exeter. He also gave us the Cathedral's history, dating back quite a few hundred years. After lunch Captain Appleyard thanked everyone for their hospitality and we started back to camp feeling quite happy with our trip. It had been a most enjoyable weekend and a break from the monotony of camp life.

Although we were at one time stationed near Canterbury Cathedral in Kent, I never did get to see the inside of it. We also had a Church Parade at Chichester Cathedral when we were stationed nearby on Sir Bernard Epstein's estate.

Before we left Toronto, we had deposited our Regimental colours in St. James Cathedral, where I expect they remain. We received new Colours while in England.

When I was wounded in Normandy, Captain Appleyard was at the Field Dressing Station I was taken to. I was in shock but had been given a painkiller, so wasn't feeling too bad. I asked him when he was going to have another padre's tour. He smiled and said he would let me know. After the war he went on to become a Bishop.

I also got to see the Tron Kirk on High Street in Edinburgh, as well as the Castle and Holyrood Palace, all of which, as the saying goes, are 'steeped in history' – some of it quite grim.

Chapter Eleven

HOUSEY-HOUSEY
('You're in the Navy Now')

While training on the Isle of Wight, we made two trial landings on the mainland. The 'mother ships' that we used were Channel Ferries that had been fitted out with landing craft. This exercise was carried out at night, and on the first try, our navigator did not make quite enough allowance for the tide or drift or something. We landed a mile or two past our designated area. We stormed ashore (actually most of us crawled across the shingle on our hands and knees) and proceeded inland. We had been issued a rum ration on the ship. Some of us gave ours to Nappy Lesarge, a tough little character from the North. By the time we had crossed the beach, Nappy was out like a light. Not to worry. The referee labelled him our first casualty and two medics put him on their stretcher and hustled him off to a First Aid Post. It was daylight now, and we finally got our bearings and proceeded down into the village we were supposed to have captured. We were greeted by the Home Guard with their array of unorthodox defence weapons, most of which they had constructed themselves. They congratulated us on our brilliant strategy of outflanking them.

On our second landing I was in the advance party and had to remain on the mother ship in Yarmouth or Bournemouth harbour. There were two of us privates and a sergeant – Sgt. Kay, I think his name was. I remember that he was from Niagara Falls and no doubt had been R.C.R. trained as I had been. I was detailed to pick up our rations from the galley while we were aboard ship. On my first attempt, the sailor who was dishing out the rations asked 'How many, mate?' I held up three fingers and he got a large tray and started putting fifteen lots of rations on it. I tried to explain that there were only three of us. The sailor said: 'You're in the Navy now, mate. You order your rations by table in the navy and one table seats five sailors.' For the rest of our stay aboard ship I held up one finger and drew rations for five each meal, to include cigarettes. When we left the ship, our packs were stuffed with biscuits, tea, sugar, Grey Nun cigarettes and whatever else we couldn't eat.

All the time we were on the ship there was a continuous bingo game being held on the mess deck. The sailors called it 'housey-housey'. The caller gave his own version of the numbers that came up. For instance sixty-six would be 'clickety-click' and so on. By the time I had learned just what the hell he was talking about, it was time for us to go ashore. We had not won anything in the housey-housey game but still had all those extra rations the Navy had so kindly donated.

The next time we went aboard the mother ship, we were

visited by Lord Louis Mountbatten, Chief of Combined Operations. He told us that we were going to raid the coast of France. We would be given plenty of air support and possibly some paratroops. There was another naval officer with him, who gave a brief run-down on a New Year's Day raid on the Lofoten Islands or some other unlikely spot. He stressed the importance of surprise. On this particular raid, the German troops had been celebrating since Christmas. The raiding party commandos were the only ones that were surprised – all they found were empty bottles.

The next morning, at six o'clock prompt, when the ack-ack crews were changing, the lights went on and then off. This was followed by WHAM WHAM! two loud explosions. We had been sleeping in hammocks below deck. R.S.M. Murry, a real tough little World War One veteran, jumped up from his cot in one corner and yelled: 'Steady men, steady' in a stern voice. I was tempted to add 'We always are ready' but decided to keep my mouth shut. Some joker – and we had our share of them – said 'Go on back to bed, old timer.' The R.S.M. yelled in a sterner voice: 'Who said that?' He was greeted by a chorus of 'He did. Put him on the peg.' That meant charge him, whoever he was, with 'moppery', I guess.

We scrambled on deck after carefully folding our hammocks as the Sgt. Major had instructed us when he was tucking us in the night before. On deck we learned that we had been attacked by one plane carrying two bombs or by two planes each with one bomb. Both of our ships had received a hit or near miss, but we were still afloat and not in danger of sinking. The only casualty that I can remember on our ship was a friend of mine, Alan 'Tommy' Tomlinson from the 'I' Section. He had been in the heads when the bomb struck and had bumped his knee on a urinal. I said he was lucky that was all he bumped, having been caught in such an exposed position. Tommy made a full recovery. I saw him back in Canada early in 1945. He had volunteered to go to Japan. I wondered if maybe he had bumped his head that morning on the ship.

Incidentally, our raid was postponed and we went back to the mainland to a place called Seven Oaks – or was it Eight Elms?

I was sent on leave and told to report back to our Holding Unit. When I arrived back there, I found that their Quartermaster was my old sergeant from 'A' Company, Jerry Simmonds. He thought it was about time that I had a complete new outfit, two of everything. I went back to the regiment with a draft of replacements. The Regiment was being re-built after the Dieppe disaster, and with all my new outfit I blended in with the rest of the recruits. After a few weeks Capt. Graham McLaughlin, who had been in charge of the 'I' Section when I was in it, asked me if I would like to be a lance-corporal. I wasn't sure that I could stand the responsibility but decided to give it a try. A lance-corporal in the New Royals was expected to be Guard Commander, Orderly Sergeant and whatever else was needed. After a few months of this, with no more stripes being handed out, I asked for a transfer. I was sent to the Bren Gun Carrier Platoon in Support

Company. Capt. Waters was our Company Commander and the Sergeant was Glen Lewis, whom I had known back in 'A' Company. They tried to make a corporal out of me without success. I was quite content to be a bren gunner. The bren gun was easier to tote than the old Lewis Gun and didn't have as many parts to foul up. Also, with the carriers, we always had plenty of ammo handy, a tarp to use as a tent if necessary, a small stove for making tea and a small wireless set. Sometimes we could get German music from Calais, and that is where I first heard 'Lili Marlene', which became the top song of W.W.2. I think even Vera Lynn was singing it before the War ended.

Chapter Twelve

THE WHIRLY BIRD

In the spring of 1944 we were at the Kent Flying Club, waterproofing our bren carriers. There were special troughs built for the final testing. There was a small hangar at one end of the field, and the old runways had row upon row of concrete posts to discourage any plane from trying to land on them. It was a beautiful sunny day and all was quiet, even in the skies.

Suddenly a small aircraft appeared high overhead. We could see that there was something different about this plane, but we were not sure just what it was. The pilot made a wide circle to lose altitude and came in for a landing between two rows of the posts. The plane taxied to a stop and a Yankee officer stepped out. 'I was expecting these stupid sheep to get out of my way,' said the pilot. We pointed out to him that the 'sheep' he had seen were concrete posts. He laughed and said: 'They sure looked like sheep to me.' He had been testing this new plane, called a Whirlwind, and it had developed engine trouble. It looked much larger on the ground. The difference that we had failed to spot was that it had twin fuselages and tail assemblies. The officer asked where he could find a telephone, and we went back to our work.

The next morning, when we arrived at the Flying Club, there was a convoy of American Army trucks already there. They dismantled the Whirlwind and carted it off in their vehicles. I never saw another aircraft like it in England or anywhere else. Did you? We always referred to it as 'the whirly bird'.

Chapter Thirteen

INVERARY – THE COLDEST PLACE EVER

Late in 1943 the Royals were sent to Inverary on the west coast of Scotland for more Special Training. I was sent on the advance party. I didn't volunteer, I was just detailed. When we arrived at Inverary, the group that had been there ahead of the Royals were on their last day's training. It was a cold wet day with an icy wind blowing in from the sea. Their task was to climb a wicked looking trail up a rather steep mountain. Not my idea of a pleasant outing! When they returned, I got talking to some of them over a few beers. They described the trail and what was at the top in detail, including exactly where to find 'Kilroy Was Here' carved. When the rest of our boys arrived, I told some of them that I had climbed up the hill with the previous group and described the top in detail – before I forgot.

The camp was operated by English Garrison Engineers and they were allowed two men from each new group for fatigue duties around the camp. As there were only two of us and an N.C.O. on the advance party, we were chosen. They issued us with leather jerkins (Robin Hood style) like those they all wore, and outlined our duties. Mainly we had to keep the Garrison Lecture Hall tidy. After the first lecture in the morning, we would clean the place up. As we had at least an hour before the next lecture would be over, we would head for the tearoom in the village. There was seldom anyone else around, so we would sit in the only two chairs by the fireplace and enjoy the tea. One morning an Army truck stopped outside the tearoom and an English Brigadier (Red Tabs and all) and his driver came in for a spot of tea. They had sort of taken us by surprise, so we just sat and quietly sipped our tea. They stood behind us, gulped down their tea, and went on their way. We finished our tea and went back to camp, wondering if we should have been a bit more polite and offered our seats. After that incident we still went for our morning tea and sat by the fire, but were never as relaxed as before.

The weather was bad all week, cold rain, sleet and very windy. The Royals were always cold and wet when they returned each evening. The best we could do was to make sure there was plenty of hot tea ready when they came back.

On the last day after returning from climbing that mountain, most of the boys said that it hadn't been too bad. They also said that they really hadn't believed that I had been up there until they had checked out my description of exactly where 'Kilroy Was Here' had been carved.

I think that we were all glad to see the last of Inverary and the Duke of Argyle's castle. He had long before stopped the troops from having a peek inside – too many souvenir hunters.

We arrived back at Denne Park on Christmas Eve, to find that the boys who had been left to guard the camp had already started their holiday celebrations. They were having a party in the Nissen hut that our platoon used, and it was in a rather messy state. However, they tidied things up a bit and invited us to go over to the Fox and Hounds with them to continue the party. We all had another pleasant Christmas, our last in England.

Chapter Fourteen

INSPECTIONS

Of all the various times that we were inspected by Army Brass and dignitaries, the one that I remember most was when His Majesty King George VI and Sir Anthony Eden inspected the Royals fairly early during our stay in England. We were stationed in Aldershot and the inspection took place at nearby 'Boo Hill', so named because on some occasions we would all be camouflaged by the roadside. At the appropriate moment we would all jump up with a loud shout. It was quite impressive, I'm sure, but seemed to be what was expected of 'Colonial Troops'. We didn't do this for the King, as it was a more formal inspection. We had done a lot of training for this inspection and our Canadian-made uniforms were still in good shape. I think that the King was impressed by our turnout. He was especially interested in 'Royal', our Great Dane mascot, and had his picture taken with him. I think this picture appeared on the Humane Society calendar in Canada the following year.

Some time later we were inspected by General (later Field Marshal) Sir Bernard Montgomery. It was after his great victory at El Alamein in the desert. He was very

51

enthusiastic in his speech, and very optimistic about our role in the coming invasion of Europe. He had us break ranks and gather around him – we had been told to expect this. He did not dwell on his past success, but on what he intended to do – with our help – to win the war.

His personal life was quite tragic. He had lost his wife to some rare disease while she was still quite young.

The Royals were also inspected by General Eisenhower after he became Commander-in-Chief of all the Allied Forces. There were two weeks of special guards training before we were presented with new Regimental Colours. I must have been on leave because I missed it. I did get to see the ceremony and to join in the party that we had afterwards.

On one occasion we were followed on an inspection parade ground by half a dozen stray dogs. I guess they just wanted to see our mascot, 'Royal'. Our Commanding Officer took rather a dim view of this, because the dogs had to be rounded up (and coralled) before the inspection could proceed. I think some of the boys must have lost their temporary pets, as it never happened again.

The last inspection I can remember was Kit Inspection on the parade ground, a special at which we were relieved of all our surplus kit – or most of it.

Chapter Fifteen

THE AIR MATTRESS

The first year that we were in England Marie had sent me an air mattress. It was khaki in colour and had six compartments and a separate pillow. This made it easy to inflate by mouth. Of course some of the jokers would say that they could tell when it had enough air in it by the colour of my face. It could be folded up to the size of a groundsheet. I kept it out of sight during the day, not taking any chances with pranksters.

Early in 1944 we were each issued with a special kit bag. We were told that anything we wanted to keep, such as souvenirs etc., were to be put in this kit bag, which would be stored in a depot in England. I thought that in war time it was generous of the army to bother. I had a few things from Iceland and Scotland that I wanted to keep, and there was still plenty of room in the bag for my air mattress. Some of the boys watched me fold it carefully and stow it in the kit bag. They wondered how I was going to sleep without my air mattress.

We had been warned several times not to keep anything that wasn't army issue. One morning we were told to fall in in 'Full Marching Order'. There was always plenty of speculation and rumours about our next move, so we were ready for almost anything. Anything, that is, except a Kit Inspection on the parade ground yet. Some of us had to return to our tents for missing items. While the Kit Inspection was going on, a Special Detail – they must have been M.P.'s – went through our tents and stripped them bare. Everything they found was piled in a heap on the parade ground, and then carted off in an army truck.

I can remember noticing some nice sets of brushes in leather cases on that pile of extra kit. I was sure glad that my air mattress was safely tucked away. There were a lot of sad faces around camp for a while. After a day or two the incident was forgotten. We still had a war to think about.

When we finally arrived in Normandy, and before we were assigned to an area, we had a day or two to get settled in. On the first evening in Normandy I remarked that it had been quite a long day and that I was going to bed early. I nonchalantly unfolded my air mattress and proceeded to inflate it. We sometimes used the seat cushions from our bren carriers for pillows. I had removed the stuffing from mine and had substituted my air mattress. Unfortunately, during the next few weeks we had very little time to sleep, but I did use it the first few nights. When I was wounded, my air mattress was still in our bren carrier. Years later, back in Canada, I met Alan Mann, our driver. The first thing I asked him was: 'What happened to my air mattress?' He said that he really didn't remember and that the next time he was in Germany he would look for my air mattress and his bren carrier. I wondered if he was being a bit sarcastic. I'll bet he flogged my air mattress in Brussels or Antwerp long before they reached Germany!

Chapter Sixteen

D-DAY
(On Our Way At Last)

On the morning of June 6th, 1944, we were informed over the speaker in our camp that the Allied Forces had landed in France. We were stationed in Kent, north of Dover. We had been on alert most of the night because of low-flying planes over our area. There was always the threat of paratroops landing. In the morning we could see small planes streaking across the sky in the general direction of London. Later in the day we learned that they were Hitler's new V-One 'Buzz Bombs'. They were small planes without pilots travelling on a beam set for London. When they ran out of fuel, they crashed and their bomb exploded. Sometimes you could hear an engine suddenly cut-out and then an explosion, but always in a distant area.

A few weeks later, when we set out for Normandy, we went through the tunnel under the River Thames at Woolwich. The buzz-bombs had done considerable damage in that area, but not as far north as the Tilbury Docks, where we were going to embark on our L.C.T., headed for Normandy.

While waiting to go to France, we had been completing our training in the beautiful Kent countryside. We were allocated a certain amount of petrol for training purposes. We would pick a spot on a map, a town or village, divide our bren carriers into three groups, and then approach our target from different angles, cross country if necessary. In most of the villages there would be a tea room, which we would converge on to make our Headquarters and plan

our route back to camp. Sometimes there would be a fireplace in the tea room and you could make a slice of toast to have with your tea.

We also did a certain amount of night training. One night one of our bren carriers overturned and one of the crew was killed. I don't remember his name; he hadn't been in the Carrier Platoon very long. I do remember that he was supposed to be going on a weekend pass the next day. That was one of the few accidents we ever had in England with the bren carriers. Considering the winding roads and the narrow streets through the many villages, this was no small feat.

Chapter Seventeen

BREAK OUT OR BREAK UP

The Royals had been in Normandy since July 6th. We had watched the Lancasters' low-level daylight bombing of Caen. What I remember most was seeing the air-crews bailing out when their planes were hit. There was an off-shore breeze, and they were being carried out to sea by the wind. Of course the Air Sea Rescue launches were dashing around plucking them out as fast as they could.

Later, when we passed through Caen, there was nothing left but rubble. Some of the boys were sitting in their carriers with their feet in the air to show off their pointed-toe French shoes. It wasn't considered looting; the contents of the stores were scattered all over the streets.

Our place in the line was near a river and was under mortar fire most of the time, especially at night, when the Germans would move their small mortars up closer. We kept digging our slit-trenches deeper and sand-bagging the entrance. One of the boys left his ammo pouches outside and they were blown to bits. We had a few casualties, including our Medical Officer. There were a number of tall trees around, and some of the mortar bombs would explode when they hit the branches. That was fine until the trees ran out of branches. Needless to say, we got very little sleep. We would line up our hand grenades at dusk and wait. At first some of the newer recruits didn't know they had to put detonators in their grenades, but we soon explained that little detail. We never did have to use our grenades while I was there, but I came close.

It was a foggy sort of night and I was about half asleep. Suddenly I could see two shadowy figures advancing towards me. They were still well out of grenade-throwing range, but I grabbed a grenade and was ready to pull the pin. The shadowy figures kept slowly coming on, starting and stopping until they decided to change direction. Then I could see that they were cows grazing. I was sure glad that I hadn't panicked and put our whole line on alert, besides giving away our exact position. On one of the quieter afternoons we could hear shells swishing across behind our lines. There were some tanks parked on our right and beyond that the ruins of some houses. The crew of a German 88 artillery gun had hidden their weapon in one of the basements of the houses and had been bypassed in the advance. Now they had decided to open up on the tanks. We soon learned what it was all about when the shells started hitting the tanks and the crews started bailing out. The tanks that hadn't been hit quickly converged on the Eighty-Eight and silenced it. I'll bet they also checked the rest of the basements.

On another occasion a small scout car drove along behind our lines, followed by a row of mortar bombs. The English officer calmly left his vehicle and walked back and apologized to one of our officers for having drawn mortar fire on our position. On another occasion one of our support regiments sent out a rather large fighting patrol. They crossed a little to the right of our line but must have returned by a different route.

After a few days (it seemed much longer) we were relieved by the Essex Scottish of our Brigade. The change was made at night and everything was going smoothly until we were passing through our artillery, which was located behind our lines. A few German planes, Heinkel Medium Bombers, picked this particular time to stir things up a bit. First they dropped flares and then circled to pinpoint their targets. It looked to us as if each plane was directly over our heads. Of course we were out of our bren carriers and into the ditches without delay. We did have one casualty, a chap named Drysdale, who was hit in the shoulder by a bomb fragment. After things had quietened down, somebody directed us to a First Aid Post. We took our wounded man in a carrier to have him looked after. It wasn't far to the First Aid Post, but when we got there we were told that the road we had used had not yet been cleared of mines. Most of the mines had been placed on the verges, the sides of the roads. The real danger was when two vehicles were passing, so were were lucky we didn't meet any other vehicles.

The only other action I can remember was when the Royals were called on to take out a large chateau and orchard at the village of Louvigny. There was a high stone wall around the orchard and the German S.S. Panzer troops that were defending it were well dug in. The bren carrier platoon was brought in to consolidate the position after it had been captured following upon a fierce battle. Some of the boys stretched out in that orchard had been friends of mine for four years. Another thing I noticed was how young some of the German casualties looked – Hitler Youth I suppose. When I was in our hospital in England, there was one German lad there. He was about fifteen years old and had been on the Russian Front before being sent to Normandy. He said he wasn't really a German, because he was from the free city of Danzig, but had been drafted into the German Army.

On the morning of July 25th, 1944, the Royals were advancing, along with the rest of the Fourth Brigade of the Canadian Army. The bren carriers were on the left flank and we soon came under heavy mortar fire. 'Moaning Minnies' we called them, because of the strange sound their mortars made. We called in the Typhoon rocket-carrying planes and they came swooping down and blasted some of the mortars. I was later told that some of the German mortars were mounted on trucks, thus making them mobile targets. We had a few casualties, including one of our officers whose carrier received a direct hit. We could see the Germans running around near some haystacks a few hundred yards away. We kept firing our Bren Guns at them without much success. I tried setting the haystacks on fire with some tracers. I could hit them, but the hay must have been too green to burn. At one point I could see someone crawling along behind a hedge not far in front of us. I trained my Bren on a break in the hedge all ready to shoot, when he came into full view. It turned out to be one of our own men from C Company. I was sure glad that I had waited. Our driver had a two-inch mortar that he could fire from the carrier. He fired as many smoke bombs as he could to help us get back out of range of the enemy mortars.

There was somewhat of a lull in the action so we started digging slit trenches. I was hit by the first mortar bomb to

land in our area when the firing resumed. A medic named Scott tried to help me, but he was hit in the face. He lost an eye but lived through it. I was rushed back to the First Aid Post by two stretcher-bearers with a jeep, and later to a Field Hospital by ambulance. I knew that I had been hit in the stomach and that my left arm was hanging useless. I didn't know or care about my right foot. The last thing that I remember was being taken from the ambulance into some sort of building. There was a beautiful Red Cross nurse standing by the door. This could well have been an illusion.

When I woke up some time later, I was in a large tent full of wounded soldiers. There was a chorus of whistles coming from those things they put in your mouth after operations. I had been operated on by a team of surgeons, Doctor Eaton, an older doctor and Doctor Mills, a young doctor with red hair. Years later I saw Doctor Mills in Sunnybrook Hospital. I had a body cast for my left shoulder, a bandage on my right foot and a colostomy. There was a tube in my throat, and when I drank water it would just come back up in the tube. An orderly gave me a Damon Runyon paperback to read. Though the stories were funny, I couldn't laugh much but I still enjoyed reading them.

There was a padre who came around to see us every day. We would ask him how the war was going and he would always say, 'Fine – don't worry'. I wondered why the shelling at night sounded just as close as ever. I learned later that there were some old 'Battle Wagons' or Monitors, which, no doubt, were at Jutland with Lord Jellicoe. They would stand offshore in the daytime and then move in closer at night to bombard the German positions. They had a range of about fifteen miles and made quite a racket.

After two weeks in the Field Hospital, I was flown by Dakota from the beach near Bayeau to Swindon Airport near Winchester. I remember even getting a glimpse of the White Cliffs of Dover, and they sure looked good to me. Swindon Airport was staffed mostly by Royal Airforce W.A.A.F.S. These girls, some of them quite thin, could swing the stretchers from the plane to the ambulance. I was taken to the Canadian Military Hospital near Pinewood Studios. It was staffed mostly by doctors and nurses from the Royal Victoria Hospital in Montreal, but some of them could speak English. I had a bit of trouble explaining that my right ankle had never been properly taken care of. The nurses would tap it with their fingers and say 'cast'. I would say 'non-non' because I knew it was just dried blood with a clean bandage on it. Finally one of the doctors had a nurse cut the bandage off, clean up the foot and put a cast on. The last piece of shrapnel was removed from my foot in the old Christie Street Hospital after I had been home a few months.

Life in the hospital wasn't too bad. I remember that some of the Nursing Sisters would go to their mess and have a drink or two before starting a shift in a ward with forty stomach wounds. I could understand that, because it was summer and there was no air conditioning. It was quite hot in England that August. The main topic on the news seemed to be that some of the harvesters were going on strike because of the shortage of beer. The next most important item on the news was American General George Patton's spectacular sweep around the right flank of the Allied Line in France. It had started on July 25th, 1944, so I remember the date very well.

I walked out of the hospital with a slight limp in January

1945, and went on leave to London. The V-2's were landing on London. I didn't want to press my luck too far, so I continued on to Edinburgh. After my leave I returned to a Holding Unit. I was included in a draft of tri-wound cases from Italy who were going back to Canada on leave. If you were wounded three times, you were given a month off. I had only been wounded once – in three places, but I didn't argue about that. We came back to Canada on an American ship, and there was plenty of spaghetti, weiners and cokes on the menu. For the next ten days we re-fought the war in Italy battle by battle. Near the end of our voyage I could join in and argue whether it was the Hitler Line or some other that we were attacking that day. I also learned a few more Italian words and traded some French francs for Italian coins.

Back in Halifax, the first thing I can remember is being served bacon and eggs for breakfast on the train. It was the first time in five long years.

Chapter Eighteen

HOME AGAIN

Our train arrived at Toronto's Exhibition Grounds on February 14th, 1945. Marie was waiting, but she had a little difficulty in recognizing me because I had lost so much weight. I was given a month's holiday and told to report back to the C.N.E. Grounds. There were a few of us waiting to be discharged. As there didn't seem to be any rush, I started going on Sick Parade every morning. On March 31st, 1945 I was given my Discharge Certificate and told that I would be receiving a Disability Pension which amounted to $50.00 a month.

Marie was working on Lancaster bombers for A.V. Roe at Malton. She was in the Flight Test department, and was one of the few girls ever to get a ride in a Lancaster. She didn't work too long after I was home. After about a month of resting and buying some new clothing, I thought I had better start looking for a job. I registered at the Unemployment Insurance Office on Spadina Avenue and was sent to the old Toronto Police Headquarters at 149 College Street for a job as a clerk. I was interviewed by the Chief Constable, Brigadier-General Dini Draper. He asked me what regiment I had served in and said that he knew some of the officers in the Royal Regiment. Then the Chief leaned over his desk, shook my hand and said: 'Welcome to the Toronto Police Force.' I was assigned to the Property Office, which was open twenty-four hours a day. I had started playing golf again at the Humber Valley Golf Course. Sometimes, if I was working the night shift, I would play golf in the morning. One of the Police Cadets, Harold Wilson, would sometimes go golfing with me. Harold knew some of the detectives who were golfers, and got us an invitation to play at the Rosedale Golf Club.

It was the nicest golf course I had ever played. The pro, Jim Johnston, was a friend of some of the police. I think that we were the only ones ever allowed to play there who weren't at least members of the National Club on Bay Street. We also played in the Police Golf Tournaments that were held at the Cutten Field Golf Club in Guelph. I stayed with the Toronto Police Department five years and then moved on, first to the Finance Department, where I stayed until 1982. I still get a small government annuity for my years with the Toronto Police Force.

I played in some of the City Hall Golf Tournaments. One year we had a match-play tournament at Tam O'Shanter Golf Club. In my first match I played a young chap who was a good golfer. After the first three holes, he was one under par, but was down two holes. I hung on to my lead to win that match and all the others up to the final. My friend Don McIntee beat me in the final. I received a nice carving set for being runner-up. While in the Militia, we had a golf day at the West Hill Golf Club. I won a plaque for the low gross.

Playing the Humber Valley Course, 1945.

In November, 1945, I watched the Royals march proudly up University Avenue to the Armory to be disbanded. There were still a few who had been with us in 1940. Paddy Ryall was one. He was now a Major and Second-in-Command of the Regiment. He had been our Platoon Sgt. Major back in the Exhibition Grounds.

I had one hole-in-one while playing the Humber Valley course. It was a blind shot and rather low, so I thought it would go over the green. My wife could see the green from the ladies' tee and said, 'I think it's in,' and it was. Next time I hope I can see the shot myself.

STATEMENT OF SERVICE
In the
CANADIAN ARMED FORCES

Name:	William Emanuel GIRARD
Service Rank or Number:	B-66590
Branch of Service:	Canadian Army (Active)
Date and Place of Birth:	10 April 1917 Chandler, Que.
Date and Place of Appointment, Enlistment or Enrolment:	8 September 1939 Toronto, Ont.
Date and Place of Retirement or Discharge:	30 March 1945 Toronto, Ont.
Type of Retirement or Discharge:	Honourable
Rank on Retirement or Discharge:	Private
Remarks:	Also served from September 1933 to April 1935 in the Canadian Army (Militia)

24 July 1995
Date

Director, Personnel Records Centre

Statement of Service received on retirement.

71

Chapter Nineteen

RE-TREADS

In late 1960 I was in Sunnybrook Hospital for a check-up. There were a few other Royals there too and they told me about the Regiment preparing for its One Hundred Years' Anniversary in 1962. I had rather lost contact – too busy raising a family, but decided to look into it. The result was that I joined up again in the Royal Regiment Militia, Support Company. At least this time I was joining, not The Royal Canadian Regiment, but The Royal Regiment, and I knew it.

There were quite a few old Royals – called 're-treads' – joining up. One of them was Johnny Travers, whose dad, Jock, had been in the Lincoln and Welland way back in 1933 A.D. Johnny's favourite expression was 'Damn my sister's cat's ass', which he could apply to any given situation, especially to impress the younger lads. I have never heard this expression used by anyone else, even back in Fort Erie.

There were all kinds of Special Events going on in the Royal Regiment. One was a jaunt to Saskatchewan, which I missed. It was to commemorate the Battle of Batoche. They went by plane this time. The first time was by rail, plus marching the last hundred miles. At least one of the Royal Regiment returned minus his dress uniform.

We also had a Trooping of the Colour on the back campus of the University of Toronto, and took part in the Pageant at the C.N.E. Grandstand. Another year we led the Warriors' Day Parade at the Exhibition. The final event that I can remember was the banquet at the King Edward Hotel. I still have the special glass they gave us.

Some of us re-treads decided to stick around for a few years. One year Support Company won an award for being the best Company in the Regiment. These were the Diefenbaker years, and we were given special training. It included crowd control, rescue tactics and other training. I learned how to tie a few knots, never having been in the Boy Scouts. Some of the six-week courses didn't require you to be in the militia, and they paid standard army pay. One W.W.2 old soldier told me that he had taken the course three times under different names. It was a change from the regular militia training. I also took a few other militia courses, N.C.O. and Signals, and ended up an acting-sergeant, too old to be confirmed.

On June 25th, 1965, the Toronto Scottish Regiment was presented with new Colours by Her Majesty, The Queen Mother. The presentation was made at Varsity Stadium and a few Royals went to help fill in one of the Guards. I was in the rear rank near the end of the line and was in one of the pictures of Her Majesty, The Queen Mother. This photo was published in the *Canadian Army Journal*, Vol. XIX, No. 2.

The Royals had a Parachute Jumping Club operating

In the Militia, aged 50.

while I was there, but I was a bit too old for that. However, one year at Camp Petawawa I did make a few jumps from a Twin Otter – but only after it had landed. I think the Parachute Club was run by Capt. MacDonald, our Support Company Commander.

I remained in the Militia (Reserve Forces) until I reached the age of fifty, the compulsory retiring age.

74

Canadian Army
Certificate of Military Qualification

B 812606
SERVICE NUMBER

Private
RANK

GIRARD W
NAME

R REGT C
UNIT

having completed the required training, has qualified as

Militia Junior NCO

Canadian Army - Militia
COMPONENT OF ARMY

28 Feb 63
EFFECTIVE DATE

by authority of

for (G Kitching)
Major General
General Officer Commanding
Central Command

Canadian Army Certificate of Military Qualification, 1963.

Chapter Twenty

CAPTAIN (NAVAL) ANDY POPIEL

I was working at the City Hall, City Clerk's Department, most of the time I was in the Militia. A young Polish lad joined the Department and we became good friends. He had led a very interesting life. His father had been a Colonel in Cavalry. They had lived on a large estate and his father had supplied most of the mounts for his regiment. As everyone knows, the Polish cavalry lasted only a few days against the German Panzers and Stuka dive bombers.

Andy's father escaped to Italy and took Andy with him. His father served in the 8th Army in Italy. After the War they came to Canada. They settled in the Eastern Townships of Quebec. His father bought a farm and started raising horses again.

Some time while growing up, Andy had worked on ships and held a Master's Certificate. I don't think he ever tried to use it in Canada. Andy joined the Royals and brought a few of his Polish friends with him. They could all drink vodka straight, or, as we say, neat. The first night Andy came on parade he met one of our officers who was from Liechtenstein and who had known Andy's father. After our

parade, he invited Andy to the Officer's Mess. I had been around for a few years and was lucky to get into the Sergeants' Mess. I didn't mind too much because he was such an interesting character. He was also invited to the Royal Military Institute a few times.

Andy didn't stick around Toronto too long. There wasn't enough action for him at City Hall. He dropped in to see me one time after he had left. He had joined Air Canada, or whatever it was called back then. He was in Public Relations and had been sent to Warsaw to investigate the possibility of opening an office there. He insisted that he be allowed to wear an Air Canada uniform while he was in Poland. I asked him how he was treated in Poland and he said, 'like an aristocrat,' which I think he was. He told them he was a General Public Relations man in Air Canada. He really wasn't around the Royals long, but I'll bet that he is remembered more than I am.

Chapter Twenty-One

MOVING THE BOOK OF REMEMBRANCE

(from the Old to the New City Hall)

It must have been some time in 1966 that Capt. MacDonald and I were chosen as the Royal's representative when the book containing the Honour Roll Of Remembrance For War Veterans was moved from the Old to the New City Hall. Capt. MacDonald had the honour of carrying the Book. I was in the escort, which was made up of one representative from each Unit in the Military District. A Chief Petty Officer from the Navy was in charge of the escort.

I obtained two copies of a photo of this event from the *Toronto Star*. I gave one of the photos to Capt. MacDonald and still have the other one. The Book of Remembrance is in the main lobby of the New City Hall. It is in quite an impressive setting and worth a look, next time you are at the City Hall.

Chapter Twenty-Two

2736 ROYAL REGIMENT OF CANADA CADETS

Back on Civvy Street in 1969, I was spending more evenings at home with my children and Marie was working as a nurse. I received a letter from Major Rob Howard, an officer in the Royals. He was trying to complete his education while working as a Toronto Fire Fighter. He was looking for someone to help him with the Royals Cadets. In the Army Cadets an instructor was allowed to continue after reaching the age of fifty. I had been recommended to him by a mutual friend, George Graves, one of the Old Royals. I thought I might as well have one last fling, so agreed to give it a try. I was commissioned as a Second Lieutenant, and after one year was promoted to the rank of Lieutenant. We had a fine group of about fifty young Cadets.

We did regular training, including drill, weapons training and First Aid. We also went on bus trips to places like Fort George at Niagara-on-the-Lake, and took part in some out-of-town parades. One time while we were waiting for a bus, someone tried to get a sing-song started. We tried all the old war songs without much response. So

then we tried the Mickey Mouse song and the Cadets all joined in enthusiastically, which shows that you have to change with the times.

My son Paul was never interested in the army or Cadets. Once while we were attending a Christmas Party at the Fort York Armory, I showed him our mortars and other weapons. His response was, 'Do you have any three-stage rockets?'

We had a Pioneer Section like the Regiment's, maybe not quite as large. On one road trip we left one of our silver-plated axes, which the Pioneers carried on a bus. Luckily I was able to track it down through the T.C.C. On another occasion we stopped our bus at the scene of an accident and some of the Cadets were able to assist with First Aid.

When I joined the Cadets we didn't have any type of flag or banner. I set about trying to remedy this situation. After scrounging some funds from the Regiment and Association we came up with a banner. Just in time still to include the Union Jack in one corner. With our new Canadian Flag and a Province of Ontario Flag, we now had a Colour Party for inspections and parades. Major Homfray Clifford, the Royals Padre, came to one of our parades officially to dedicate our new Banner and Flags.

I enjoyed being in the Cadets, but by now my daughters Suzanne and Michelle were both attending The University of Guelph. I had to concentrate more on my work. So after an army career that had spanned thirty-seven years of my life, I was placed on the Reserve List.

Chapter Twenty-Three

THE ROYAL CANADIAN MILITARY INSTITUTE

When I joined the 2736 Royal Regiment of Canada Cadets and received the rank of Lieutenant, I became eligible for membership in The Royal Canadian Military Institute. At that time I was working at the City Hall. The fact that the Institute was on University Avenue made it quite handy for me to use it for lunches and entertaining. My wife and daughter and I also enjoyed going to the Christmas Buffets. They were always something special.

After I retired from the City Hall in 1982, I didn't get to the Club as much. In 1989 we moved to St. Catharine's and after moving, I seldom ever came to Toronto. I have one of the Commemorative Plates that were issued for the one hundredth anniversary of The Royal Canadian Military Institute. I suppose my name is on the wall of the main bar, along with a few thousand others.

Sometimes, if the Military Institute was closed for a few weeks in the summer, the members were allowed to use the facilities of the Board of Trade Club, the University of Toronto Faculty Club, and the Royal Canadian Yacht Club.

I resigned from the Royal Canadian Military Institute in 1994, but there is always the possibility of my being reinstated at some future date.

I am still a member of the Royal Regiment of Canada Officers' Association, and a Life Member of the Royal Regiment of Canada Association and the Fort York Branch 165, the Royal Canadian Legion.

Chapter Twenty-Four

MEDALS, DECORATIONS AND BADGES

I received the five standard Stars or Medals for my service in the Canadian Army. They are, in the order I have them Court Mounted:-

1939-1945 Star (Canadian)
France-Germany Star (Canadian)
King George VI Defence of Britain Medal
1939-45 Canadian Volunteer Service Medal
   (with Maple Leaf Clasp)
King George VI Service Medal

I qualified for the Canadian Long Service Medal but never got around to applying for it. I was thinking about joining a Procrastinators' Club, but I keep putting that off too.

We missed out on the Atlantic Star because we didn't stay in Iceland the required six months. When we were first in England, we wore the Alabaster Force insignia, a Polar Bear, as shoulder badges. Later on we were issued the blue Second Canadian Division badges. By 1944 we had accumulated five long service chevrons. They were

In full-dress uniform with medals.

white for 1939 and red for the other years, and were worn on the lower left sleeve of our battle dress jacket.

After the war we received a metal Canadian General Service lapel badge.

While in the Militia after the war, I earned the St. John's First Aid badge and the Crossed Rifles for shooting.

85

STATEMENT OF SERVICE

IN THE

CANADIAN ARMED FORCES

Service Rank and/or Number   B-66590   Name   William Emanuel GIRARD

1. Branch of Service: CANADIAN ARMY (ACTIVE)

2. Date and Place of Birth: April 10, 1917   Chandler, P.Q.

3. Date and Place of Appointment, Enlistment or Enrolment: September 8, 1939   Toronto, Ont.

4. Theatres of Service: CANADA - ICELAND - BRITAIN - NORTHWEST EUROPE

5. Date and Place of Retirement or Discharge: March 30, 1945   Toronto, Ont.

6. Type of Retirement or Discharge: Honourable   CARO 1029(10)

7. Rank on Retirement or Discharge: Private

8. Medals and Decorations: 1939-45 STAR - FRANCE & GERMANY STAR - DEFENCE MEDAL - CANADIAN VOLUNTEER SERVICE MEDAL WITH CLASP - WAR MEDAL 1939-45

9. Remarks: Service with CIC

Date: May 16, 1967.

/DF

Supervisor, War Service Records Division

DVA 812 REV. (6-63)

*Statement of Service in Canadian Armed Forces,
including medals.*

Chapter Twenty-Five

SOME OF IT WAS FUN
Memories of the Canadian Army
Conclusion

One thing that I noticed, especially among the older men in the Royals I knew for several years, was that few of them ever talked about what they were going to do after the war was over. Some of the younger lads, most of whom were not married, liked to talk about their plans for the future. They were the saddest cases if they happened to receive a 'Dear John' letter and after a year or two quite a few of them did receive such letters.

There were plenty of other sad things that happened, like Louvigny and Dieppe, but, as I said at the beginning, some of it was fun.

The Regimental Marches that I can remember were:

Lincoln & Welland Regiment: The Lincolnshire Poacher (We sang it to the words: 'You won't get any of my peanuts, when your peanuts are gone'.)

Royal Regiment of Canada   The March of the British
                            Grenadiers and Here's To
                            The Maiden
                            (We sang it to the words:
                            What did we join the army
                            for? – We must have been
                            blinking well crazy.)

I can't remember the name of the other march, but some
of the words, as heard at Camp Niagara, were:-

>The RCR's are going away
>They won't be back for many a day
>When they come back there'll be hell to pay,
>Those rascal RCR's.